A Conjuring of Dandelions

Praise for A.L. Garcia

"*A Conjuring of Dandelions,* A.L Garcia's second collection of poetry, is beautiful, unsettling, compassionate, angry, but, above all else, always truthful. Her words, and the images she creates with them, take a laser light to the recesses of our psyches and the corners of our souls to reveal the hurt/hope that takes hold of our hearts. At times reminiscent of Plath, at other times Sharon Olds, Ms. Garcia's voice is ultimately her own; her unique vision will both captivate and reward her readers. Highly recommended."

— MICHAEL DECONZO, AUTHOR OF *WELCOME TO THE ARCADE* AND *TWO NICKELS*

"A haunting journey through heartbreak and healing, A Conjuring of Dandelions transforms pain into beauty and beauty into words. A.L. Garcia's talent for dark poetry is evident on every page of her debut collection."

— C.E. WALLACE, AUTHOR OF *JUEGO DE PALABRAS*

"Garcia has never disappointed in the realm of her writing, and she certainly holds nothing back with a collection that will sit you down and speak to you like a hidden friend in the darkest corners of your room...Garcia's prose will stop your heartbeat with one statement at a time."

— DESIDERIA MESA, AUTHOR OF
BINDLE PUNK BRUJA

"A.L. Garcia's *Dandelions* not only calls the reader to consider natural beauty and its mutability, but also the way the modern world can dim even the most beautiful things with its dark hands. Many of these poems deal with the bruises and trauma life brings. Yet, like the dandelion's fairy wands, the body, too, resists: it sheds its seeds to bring forth life, refusing to be silenced or contained."

— ANDREW K. CLARK, AUTHOR OF
JESUS IN THE TRAILER

A Conjuring of Dandelions

A POETRY COLLECTION

A.L. GARCIA

EDITED BY
CASSANDRA L. THOMPSON

Quill & Crow

A Conjuring of Dandelions:
A POETRY COLLECTION
Written by A.L. Garcia
Edited by Cassandra L. Thompson
Published by Quill & Crow Publishing House

Cover Design by Mitch Green and Fay Lane

Interior by Cassandra L. Thompson

Printed in the United States of America

ISBN (ebook) 978-1-958228-55-5

ISBN (print) 978-1-958228-56-2

Publisher's Website: quillandcrowpublishinghouse.com

Contents

PART THREE
INCIPIT VITA NOVA
THUS, NEW LIFE BEGINS

Consecratio

FOR THE DANDELIONS

Photography by A.L. Garcia

Praefatio

FOREWORD

Even at the end of its time in bloom, the dandelion transforms as if death did not exist at all, bursting into seeds all full of wishes and fairy wands ready to be blown into the wind and feed the cycle anew. As far back as I can remember, I have loved dandelions, not only for their beauty, their crudely vibrant nature, the way they dance in the breeze, but also for their capacity to resist, persist, past efforts to eliminate them, to reduce their impact on manmade things deemed more valuable like perfect lawns, and other manicured spaces where their specific wild is unwelcome.

I too have felt and often feel out of place among our status symbols of old, the pressure to conform, contort stardust to fit the frames, the images, the molds held in high esteem. We are persuaded, pushed and prodded too often into bartering what individuality we are born with for over-worn ideals time and again, often at threat of indifference, or violence, or myriad forms of death. What choices do we have left when dandelions with all their grace, their medicine, their fruits, their fairy wands, their wishes, all butterfly kisses, are reaped for their rewards and yet labeled weeds, ripe for slaughter in our pretty, manufactured lawns.

Are we so far from them, as daughters of this earth, this conditioning society with all conformity driven ability to drain the life, the art in us? Do we not still fancy ourselves giving trees, medicinal weeds, ripe with healing, leaving seeds to carry us, our hearts into the beckoning breeze, even at our end? I wrote and collected these poems with that feeling in my heart, with a yearning to sow my own seeds, speak my own truths once more, and maybe inspire a few unkempt roads to freedom, as dandelions do.

- A.L. Garcia, Puerto Rico, 2023

PART ONE

Ego Moriatur

I WILL DIE

and I choose death

for all

that

must

die

Ghosts Among Us

There are ghosts among us, specters of our past, anvils hidden in the ether of their legs, the silence of their anchored tongues. There are secrets in their eyes they never speak of for the fear in ours, our resistance to the messages of dead men. I know mine have stared back at them petrified, pupils dilated, irises turned stone. There were days that felt like years and years that felt like days where I would pretend to be blind, chant "you're not there, you're not actually there, you're in my head" hoping to put them to rest, unwilling to accept their dirges, songs of buried burden, generational lament intent on being solved. There are ghosts among us, dead people, corpses in discontent, walking around like regular people, just like me and you, unaware of their condition, their decomposition. They turn into monsters when you starve them, World War Z style zombies, fast as all fucking hell once they finally get a whiff of self-awareness, humanity, the effects of its gravity. They come for you faster than you could ever dream to train your mortal hooves to be, fierce as Apollo on his steed birthing daylight, horizon, a baptizing of Icarus inevitable. You fall or fly, live, die, or zombify. There are ghosts among us. I admit I see them, hear them now, admit that I always have and hope that is enough for my salvation, for resurrection.

croak

I'm going to croak one of these days
but it won't be
with some version of electronic dog collar round
my neck
leash hidden in the fog
catching wires in my periphery
short circuiting
behind great white walls
stained in a blood, a death
only I can see
I still have big arms
mad brain
strong legs
galaxies to go before I rest
I'm going to croak one of these days
I cannot rest

legs

I grew fast legs
to run from them
the voices of corpses you planted in my earth
since my forsaken birth
forced fertile knees keep pace
flee, fall, grieve, race
I crowned my feet
celestial steeds
made for galloping into the rain
towards the wild, inimitable domain
of forbidden angels
renascent tempests of a fallen empyrean
to effloresce again
awaken
much more indomitable horde than me
to be free

untitled 1

What did you aim to inculcate in me
but fear
with deplorable acts
rooted in generational pain
your carnival games
end with me
the visceral call of freedom rings
I am no product of your broken things

dancing in my room

I remember dancing in the streets of my neighborhood,
my hood
when you weren't around
I remember dancing in my room with the windows
wide open
when you weren't home
I remember the beating I took for my restless legs
when someone told you they saw me
how righteous of them to trigger your wrath
duty of man-made god no doubt
I remember you saying you could break my limbs
if you wanted
that no one would find out and if they did,
they wouldn't care
I remember I shed no tears
but the effect of your words was there all the same,
the shame

I remember silencing my hips in the beckoning breeze
wherever pious spying eyes could see
any of my "immodesty"
land of the free, home of the brave, we say
I remember closing windows despite the heat blistering
the walls
dancing in my room
it was warm as hell in there, you know
a sweltering lunacy burrowed deep into the marrow
of my bones
churning things for you to loathe
like sovereignty, honesty, joy
they are not
were never
yours or any man's to destroy

baby, cry baby doll

I remember you
feels like a million years
since I heard your voice
saw your ghost
I, as host
floating
above it all,
levitating
in the corner of that
stained popcorn ceiling
disassociating from the noise
of minefields
and birthday cake celebrations
you smiled through it all
but I remember you
baby, cry baby doll
feels like ages

since I heard your voice
that wasn't my choice
or was it?
I'm not sure anymore
but I'm sorry

bucket brain

I've
been over-honoring you
the strength you reap
resilience you display
as if those feats were anything
but by-products of pain
CHANGE FASTER
bucket brain

guts

you lost your guts again
baby doll
Can you see them?
The steaming pile
of spectral blue-green bile
regurgitated hot ass
bubbling at your feet
Can you see?
The fermented chunks
laughing
HA HA HA
at the way you weep
adorable little exorcists
you and your horde
you lost your guts again
baby doll

cow guts

tiny hands you taught
to prepare cow guts
become
the designated butcher of the family
bearing
poor metal weapons honed
chef's knife, cleaver
the small one that pares things to bone
swallows the poison in our blood
the festering wounds
how they boil, blister, pop in my gut
disgust, stomach acid
aflame in my heart
hematophagous leech enzyme preventing clots
pardon me
while I extract the rot
the doctor ordered me to be kind

show mercy
to a ghoulish little girl
you taught to prepare cow gut stew
then left to die
on the inside
I'll be in the kitchen if you need me

bang bang haiku

my mind is a loaded gun
filled with songs we've sung
bullets for my dignity

sad girl

I remember being a sad girl, void as deep as undiscovered sea hidden beneath crooked smile, rabbit teeth and that little feeling that keeps you going, not for yourself but for the ones you're convinced need you; that "I don't ever want you to know what I do, feel what I feel;" that galaxies to go before I rest; how do I leave this sunken place I engineered for survival when the only way out still shatters.

I prefer to be unheard, to smile, hold on a little while longer. I remember being a sad girl, no phase or scene or audience needed, just me, no fantasy, child of misfortune, keeper of misery.

I remember beseeching the moon to light a path, the rain to cleanse, the sea for liberty, the sun for inspiration, the willows for the strength to be a home, all on my own, the power of finding belonging in myself and no one else. I followed, galloped, blinders on, found an angry woman, rage quieted by raw logic, a trite tendency to consider points of views and the ripe reasoning of a hopeful heart paralyzed in positions of mistrust, ever at the ready, *en garde*, some weapons blunt, some sharp, poorly manufactured shield, flank of scar tissue at best.

Reminded her we were a sad emotional girl suckled at the teat of tyranny, but no tyrant were we, that wrath never solved any deity damned thing, what gods we make of stardust in our dreams all live and die by our own hand, the direction of our feet and so did she.

I remember being a sad girl.

I remember for it was I who set her free.

Who let her be.

a ghost of you

I kept a ghost of you
locked in the madhouse walls
of a decaying jester's heart
caged
unchanged
roses of hope made martyrs
blossoming morose
How often did your logic leave them for dead?
Naught but regale for the dirt beneath
fragile foundations
fed off bacchanalian greed
how often did you prefer a chalice of deceit?
over me
over the life blood I stow of bitterer truth
birthrights to freedom that I kept
cloaked in the rain I wept

there was a time I loved too
I kept a ghost of you

in absence of you

in absence of you,
your heart, your mind
I built an ancestry of earth, hovels of dirt and
dandelions
pick-pocketing time, words that rhyme, dance moves,
and everything else left abandoned by the murk of our
ill-fated coexistence
broken universe of sea glass skies,

in absence of you,
and wombs of more unforgiving trees,
I made a home of willows where the weary rest,
pillows of battered bones, bruised flesh, and sparrow's
songs.

in absence of you,
your company, its peaceless doves,

I made a mother of the moon
brethren of stars, the night that envelops them,
of dusks, with all their twilights, insights, points of
views.

in absence of you,
I found shadows of what you might have been,
we might have been,
in search of forgiving the unforgivable,
of impossibilities unbound by our history,
where we are still parts of a whole,
where I am whole,
but I was there alone.

forgiveness

I forgive you, I do
for every seed of hurt planted without permission
in our soil
it took so long for me to get here
to see
the rot for what it is
too many turns around the bold bright sun
in blind hot rage
I forgive you, I do
because the healing begins and ends with me
I am the unseen
the variable in this experiment we've called life
and I am grateful for that
wildly so
I forgive me
for holding you accountable for generations of wrong
I too, carry tainted songs

on sparrow's wings
held on to broken things too long
I forgive you, I do
because I can't love me
if I don't love you
and I do
I forgive you

just a girl

I lay your scribe to rest beside her pen, her crown
just a girl once more
same as she was before
brown eyes burnt black as sin
I lay her down to rest beside her crown
the one you oft adorned, Lisbeth
duchess of dreams, of wishing upon stars,
claiming their light
what recalcitrant resolve to war, to write
for Romulus, Remus, Rome
arrows afire
blot out the sun
our kingdom never did quite come
not the way we planned it anyway
build up the pyre one last time
for good old times, those songs we sang of auld
lang syne

let her fall
retire
plummet
back to the depths from whence she spawned
there she goes
I go
I lay her down to rest beside her pen, her crown
just a girl once more
same as she was before

woman in white

I dreamt of you last night
blurred face, woman in white
you weren't exactly yourself but some combination of
specter and paranormal force
hell bent on being seen, unwilling to be forgotten
or kept begrudgingly compartmentalized, bottled in,
contained
I have to admit I was afraid
of what you could infect with broken bloodlines
festering in the light of day
how I have preferred them out of sight, out of mind
a fallacy, in retrospect but reminder too, of things I've
kept unchanged
frozen in time, like you, your memory
blurred face, woman in white
I admit I've always been afraid of your sea glass eyes,
how they came to be, to die

how their tears dried up from all their scars
but shells of what they once were, they must have been
like those you collected, treasures for beach girls,
like us,
like me
I cried and cried and cried
I cried all night
trying to prove I'm strong enough to admit I still care
for you and what you represent
blurred face, woman in white
I am not scared
I am still me, still free, as part of you
as all the stars that burn and die in turns around
the sun
are born anew
so are we to be, brand new

lion's tooth

the poison on your tongue
it must have had some recipe for change
even you grew unaware of
to motivate
four letter sins
like rage, hate, hope, love
what thin lines between them all
some building block of antidote
held hidden in the root
longing to flower
I sprouted
fields of lion's tooth
to claim its power

untitled 2

there is no war
no weapon
no defeat
that can break me like my own
I can change that
I will
change
that

PART TWO
De Temporibus

OF THE TIMES

I intend to be
who I am
what I am
because I am

A Matter of Time

Conspiracy theories lined the sky overhead, chem-trails marring the baby blue clarity of realization rituals, storms of necromancy forming on their heels. They spawn big, dark clouds full of communion with the dead, the demons orphaned in their arms, suckled at their breasts crying out for me to remember them, to honor their survival, make their existence worthwhile. They cry rivers that go from clear to red to clear again, growl an address of grievances, wail of offense. They worry the earth with how far I've buried them beneath her soil, their lament hidden in a patchwork garden behind the cornfields seeping radioactive bile into her entrails. It's only a matter of time before it all comes bubbling to the surface, beacon for the extraterrestrial urge to chase lightning, a bolt to the chest, a spark of alchemy. No amount of tin foil on the head will save me from their reign, the way the rain reveals my heart, my mind. It's only a matter of time.

untitled 3

The only stars I've ever aimed for
are those that promise
freedom
ready my bow

i pray too

as heavy falls the evening sky
I pray
to my celestial mother for her light
my moon
to manifest
certainty under summer rain
wisdom of roots, of earth soaking my knees
pulling them down, 15 feet deep
ground and guide
my matriarch
the barbarian winds of metamorphosis
bequeath your sight
I pray too
to my celestial mother for her light

a moment in the garden

I was pulling at roots yesterday
wet, wormwood earth
flying in my eyes
birthing
transmogrifying tinctures
of salt laced sweat and dirt
seasoning epithelial cells
simmering in the summer sun
honing lessons stowed
far below
the world I've come to know
to earn
all that which lies unlearned
of Eden
to watch it burn

i don't owe you

I don't owe you proper
or prim
or penitent
I don't owe you grace
or space
to process me
past your draconian ways
I don't owe you my smiling face
or my magic laced musing heart
I don't owe you
any
of my parts

it's all alright

it's all alright
embalm me with my lips sewn shut
cotton in my mouth, my wounds
I need not final word
to defend the weight of my heart, my pounds of flesh
I need not prove myself anything other than
what carcass may expose
in undressed, un-dreaded repose
say what you need, saw at my neck
it's alright, speak for my head
cut me down to size, any matter you like
you must know by now
I've never much minded bleeding, as needed
to purge the poison in our vein
to welcome tongues, subtle as knives
it's all alright
keep my eyes pried open if you please

so I can watch in horror
as they fillet my thighs, tear them apart
to small, digestible, amenable parts
slice through my gut, spill
the soft, wet entrails over wanting desks
for all to see, to use, to scrutinize
to store in little jars
what greater ink than blood, scars
it's all alright
it's all alright
it's alright

be

I could scoop out my eyes
stop crying
lob off my tongue
stop rambling on
break cursed knees
stop running
stop falling on my ass
I could be
more of a mystery
would that make you comfortable
with me
assuage your fears
convince you
you've made a difference
saved someone
saved me
I could add stitches to my cheeks

so they don't disappoint
have some grace
as people say
joker face
make everything ok
except for me
What else would you have me be?

rubber and glue

feed
fuck
write
sleep
repeat
kill
kill
kill
the shame
the blame
the finger pointing
attention whore
cry
reply
"I'm rubber, you're glue
anything you say bounces off me

and sticks to you"
fly
high
don't give up
I'm trying

what more?

⌒◦⌒

That bitch disgust is back again
rearing her trauma bloated head
in an aftermath of sickeningly sour self-analysis
ridicule bubbling at the surface of her lips
her fancy frostbit tongue
ripe with the murder of my joyful legs
my songbird lungs
I'd like to regurgitate
the remains
of this stomach-churning bloodlust my entrails hold
for considering things from the vantage point
of my scars
my willful sacrificial lamb of a bleeding heart
won't you come down off the cross for once,
Mary, Mary, mother of woe,
crucificada

betray stigmata
what more transformation is due
pray tell
to banish the whore (my heart)
what more?

under my skin

There's something under my skin
screeching, squirming, squealing for me to listen
to trust my eyes, my ears, my instinct
in silent sister's songs
thrice blessed
thrice sold
I'm told
to peel the rose petals from under my nose
sniff out the smell of death as bloodhounds do
feed creatures undisclosed by light of day
they claw for hints of confession
for understanding motives, raw intention
exercises in deductive reasoning
digging for worms, evidence
that I am neither prey nor predator
that something pure persists

there something under my skin
but I'm not ready for it
there's something under my skin
waiting for me
to accept it

shape my spine

I shape my spine

        into this naïve

                crooked thing

      with words

full of time

        built to bow

              to worship

      the passing of ours, mine

they shine

at the base of my skull

in the dead dog dull,

the fog

tugging at tear ducts

'til rain falls

to water weeds

feed things

that should not

have

survived

I

shape

my

spine

mirror, mirror on the wall

I put my armor on piece by bloodied piece
almost in disbelief
of a need to ever do so
beneath your auric gaze
what royalty I crowned
worth worship of dauntless vein
doth yield not by decree
I can not raise my sword to thee
to that once sanctified, at all, despite it all
I polish metal flank to gold
in high heaven and infernal depth alike
see it glitter in the midday sun
alchemized, blinders on, and yet
I can not raise my sword to thee at all
In spite of walls, shield, arrow, cavalry
I yet beseech the gods

grant thee new mortar, new sand to mold, unblemished
steel
and cups of kindness
in absence of thy guard
thy dame of swords departs
I put my armor on piece by bloodied piece
almost in disbelief
of the castle glass, stone shard nestled in my wounds
mirror, mirror on the wall
have not I been the fairest of them all
no matter
I can not raise my sword to thee at all

alma soup for the soul

on the mend, I suppose
from all the stewing
skin altering peeling
of overgrown potatoes
with onions for eyes
stiff fingers still performing their rituals
with rusted blades
ever the fool
prepping, boiling guts down to broth
for the sickness
to bury it once and for all
that's all

dandelion

tell me
what cavalry you've faced
to think yourself worthy
of mangling the flowers that lie in mine
show me
what legion you possess
that could address
the ones I hoard
beneath my dainty, delicate hide
what trampling hooves dare risk their pride
burying a dandelion?

silence, please

Silence, please,
I am in need of sinking
of surrendering to the sable seraphim
their soulless swords commanding
earth swallow my remains

Silence, please, I beg
in whispers soft as kisses, sibilant
susurrus of saint and sinner alike
allow me recognize my heart again
sad, silly little sanguine star
swollen so oft with sorrow
let her die once more

Silence, please
pray, can't you see
with all your scrutinizing eyes

how I search
through scraps of galaxy for a scion
in soliloquy with sacrifice
for nearly insignificant sprouts
of all that was silenced
remains silenced

Silence, please
For the season's storms are naught
but sad simulations of who we once were
the ghosts of we saunter
scantily clad now in the summer's sun
force soft, sweet skin to scab
shed scales in serpentine fashion

Silence, please
I am in need of things suspended
unsatiated
heavy as stone in the sober light of day
what sinister sensei he's always been
all sensuality and stomp and snare
caught unaware as sleeping prey to slaughter
as much my mother's daughter as ever
am I not?

Silence, please
I am in need
of the secrets I buried in me
of subversive plots

to overcome all structure
all sarcophagi I chose to rest in
blow them to smithereens
samples of dust
because they are not what I am made of

Silence, please
I am in need
of bleeding, seething
of things lost
in simulacrum of serenity
Silence, please
I am in need

i do not pray to gods

I do not pray to gods
I pray to the moon
because she makes no promises beneath her light,
yet she is always there
Persisting, in never ending dark
I pray to the stars
Because the battles that compose them also collapse
them
and that's the only balance I've ever known
in my own
I pray to the night
urge scientific rules to bend
to justify my trust in terrifying concepts
like love
like unnatural bonds
eternal states of being and un-being
boundlessly betraying time

like the galaxies in our eyes,
the remnants of our minds
we leave behind
when flesh falls away
pound for pound of worth
all claimed by earth
ashes to ashes, dust
I do not pray to gods
I pray to the sun

PART THREE
Incipit Vita Nova

THUS, NEW LIFE BEGINS

and I choose life
for all
that deserves
to live.

Chantal

I was floating on the surface of a calm ocean one day, allowing the waves to carry me into the peace of oblivion when I heard what I can only describe as a call from the abyss. I met this girl who said her name was Chantal. She kept telling me to follow her past a row of buoys, their protection from the open sea, its dangers, its wilderness. I kept telling her it wasn't safe, looking back towards the shore but she'd just smile and beckon me again. She didn't want to go alone, I think. There was something in her eyes, a sort of melancholy blended with curiosity, and a touch of apprehension. I saw my reflection in her gaze. It was obsidian, her irises, two big round stones of black, almost like mirrors.

We treaded water. She told me she was a good swimmer, that she wasn't afraid.

i can be soil

If I lie still enough, I can be soil
ripe with earthworms
nutrient dense with decomposition
beneath the storms, the heavy skies
I can see the lightning course through my vein, my root
I can stand and be the wind, the breeze
whipping at my thighs, leather like knives
begging them not to stop
if I run fast enough, am brave enough to breathe
where air is not allowed
I can be consumed, devoured
find murder for my hostage skin, any fear still lingering
beneath
flay all my limbs, excoriate my breast, what lies within
I can condemn my lips, my tongue
fill up my mouth, my lungs
with earth

where nothing hurts, where everything is beautiful
that ever is or was or could be
I can go there, and return renewed
to the land of living
anytime I choose
because I choose life even when death vows herself my
closest friend
and I remember how she says
whether angels or devils toil
you can be soil

a place

I found a place of feeling
of healing
inside
some form of invisible cocoon, a room
where no one else resides
solitude
tepid as summer rain
auric
as the hope of alchemy
of alchemizing
morphing
from root to tip
molting skin, what roles their cells may hold
from time to time
set free from the saddle, the bridle, the rein of
expectation, duty, pride

to force evolution to fruit, to grow in the loam I'd left
abandoned
produce fields where the wild things sprout wondering
legs
and roam like they used to
I stood alone
witnessed the unfathomable
saw solid stone turn on me, crumble, brittle as bone
but I was me again
and I was free once more
in a place of feeling, a place of healing
a cocoon, a room
nothing more

two sparrows on a streetlight

I saw two sparrows on a streetlamp yesterday
and sunk
into a maelstrom of thinking
how often fortune favors
seemingly fragile things
with wings
I watched them sing
play on metal strings
no shackled sideshows near
no fear
to curdle my sight
no gags
on the liberty of flight
I saw two sparrows on a streetlight
and they reminded me of us
what we could be, have been

I didn't wait to see them part
depart
I didn't have the time
I saw two sparrows on a streetlight

indomitable things

Hope has a tendency to be
such a small but indomitable flame
oft obscured but unlost in us
in me
my hope for you is free
my faith
wild, worn, but true
as the winds have ever been
as all the times sparrows ever sing
signaling the spring
such small indomitable things
in which hope has a tendency to be
in us,
in me

horizon

alight my winged hooves
only to set thy master's limbs ablaze with sight
to scan the morphing skies
all mage in its horizon
the rolling sea
to see
her wild in me
in waves
crashing
as fall of broken chain
and shattered key
I am nothing
not one damned thing
if not free

a red sky

❧

Our mother's sky was dressed in rouge this morn
shades of pomegranate seeds
on thirsting tongues
they faded into blue
good tidings unassumed
blush of dolor forewarning
blessed storms, anew
a new day dawns
over soon to be subnivean woods
steal my heart by plundered sight
inhume eyes that stare into the sun
tears dry
no blood to bleed
pristine
I am, you are, we are
the light
the fight

a welcoming

the roots of dandelions, demons,
stir in the dead of night
their prayers sweet as song
spells of decomposition un-hushed
in most vociferous amen
I welcome them
bury me, deep
far down as your inception
for I am yours
lost without you
chained
to the broken will of logic
unleash seed of lion's teeth in me,
I beseech
horde
keep my heart kind

my mind
wild, feral, free
I welcome thee

untitled 4

When we dance

    we are not human

we are soul

    that's all I know

a requiem for longing

I ache to admit, lord
how you stir in my heart
its renascent memory
in gossamer strands
black as ink
oh, most innocent of sin
how they pull along
a requiem for longing yet
pluck strings of wayward soul
I ache to admit, lord
how you stir in my thought
beg of the stars
a will to seal my lips
silence, oh lord
my tongue,
what will for worshipping in me

in renaissance
down on my knees
I beg of thee
to silence she

a fragile thing

I find my heart a fragile thing
now and again
amidst the roaring thunder of emotion
the clanging of her swords in my defense
the beating of her drums, stomping of hooves
and battle cries of victory or loss
ever at the ready, EN GARDE
I wonder
how many whispers of faith
I've lost and have yet to lose
to the merciful mellifluous wind
how often I avoid listening
afraid of finding my heart, a fragile thing
clinging to raw resiliency
the iron grip of armor and camouflage
coddling the urge to rip it all off
stand unguarded, bare-assed

against the wild, wet willful rain and licks of lighting
lashing the heavens to find my heart
a fragile thing
again
now and again

untitled 5

To know
Were the world
With all its whipping tongues
To sully my name
Yours would defend it
In my absence
That is love

untitled 6

we do not bear joy
without the promise of nostalgia
nor hope
without the threat of all we fear
I'm still here

my dirt

the wild grass grew long legs
with wily roots
fed of the storms, rain songs, proud as thunder
beneath flowering suns
lyrics, sharp as lightning
over many moonlit deluge
the honeybees tended to the garden in my absence
held ghost till my return
I close my eyes
plunge fingers in the dirt
my dirt
my hearth
my earth

in the arms of girls

there's this saying that goes "the bigger they are, the
harder they fall"
but if you knew me at all, you'd know
my flowers, from bud to bloom,
have long learned to fear no death, no doom
for petit or grand as it may be willed to come
I've always had two green thumbs
ripe with the songs of spring and perhaps too many
tears for watering willful roots, broken things
near flawless conditions for raising giants
stars of Orion
its almost impossible not to grow, to seed, to need,
to seek
metamorphosis, of the order lepidoptera, cocoons
for what comfort tends to hush to sleep
its almost unfathomable not to weep, weaponize sorrow

borrow strength from the soil beneath my legs, my feet,
my garden, my earth
for the courage to stand tall, unbend my crooked spine
face victory, defeat, rebirth with my head held high
to free fall into dirt
crash with the weight of the whole universe, loud as
thunder, roar
path of my storms a lightning for all to see, to read,
to use
because I dream, blossom deity to worship
and yet dare to decompose as many times as needed
when evolution beckons, when the blood of God
runs cold
I close my eyes, vow journey to restore her, I alone
but when I wake, I wake in the arms of girls
wrapped tight in their iron clad embrace, their faith,
what infinite cradle of life
in the arms of girls

Acknowledgments

First and foremost, I would like to acknowledge the poets, the writers, the authors of all the books I've read or will come to read, all the poetry I've consumed and have yet to consume, to devour. You have not known what humanity, what tenacity, what hope, what self-reflection you have inspired in me in my deepest hours of need. I am primarily and at heart ever your reader, your student, and your audience. Thank you.

To Cassandra L. Thompson, for always believing in me, for gently encouraging me to write more, to delve into other forms, other genres, and for being a constant source of inspiration simply through her own consistency in writing, publishing, and uplifting other poets and writers. I am so grateful for your devoted little black heart, for your unmatched and unrivaled presence in my universe, and your wild, wonderful friendship. I am ever at your service *(the horde proclaims in the voice of thirty-six legions, huzzah!)*.

To Marie Casey, for being an unwavering source of kindness, support, friendship, all the emo vibes, and for making art that sets my whole soul on fire. Thank you also for being the first person I trusted to read this collection and for your immensely appreciated feedback. I wolf you.

To the crows, the community of poets over at Quill & Crow as well as anyone that has partaken in the monthly poetry prompts, I am so thankful for your words. They have impressed and moved me time and again and have always inspired evolution in my own. Thank you.

And last but certainly not least, to anyone who took the time to read this book, to anyone who has taken the time to read any of my work, whether in print or online, anyone who has ever commented on the poems I post, enjoyed any I have written or recited, etc., I am eternally grateful and honestly, from the bottom of my heart, simply and ever humbly at your service.

About the Author

A.L. Garcia is an Ecuadorian-American poet and writer from New York but currently based out of Puerto Rico. She studied sociology and social science at Towson University and is an army veteran. She began writing poetry as a youth in attempts to cope with tragic family dynamics. She joined the writing community in 2020 after self-publishing a personal narrative, **Broken Things**, concerning the abuse she endured as a child, and subsequently a poetry collection titled **Broken Heart Mosaics.** You can find more of her work featured in several Quill & Crow Publications.

Thank You For Reading

Thank you for reading *A Conjuring of Dandelions*. We deeply appreciate our readers, and are grateful for everyone who takes the time to leave us a review. If you're interested, please visit our website to find review links. Your reviews help small presses and indie authors thrive, and we appreciate your support.

Other Poetry Titles by Quill & Crow

Crow Calls Volume I

Rise of the Dark Goddess

Crow Calls Volume V